The Place That Keeps Love Alive

The Place That Keeps Love Alive

Coralie Shawn

www.coralieshawn.com

The Place That Keeps Love Alive

N
W **E**
S

4. Healing Where There Was Hurt:
Finding My North Star Home

Start

1. The Sun Rises East:
Chasing Dawn With You

3. The Sun Sets West:
He Left Glass Shards Behind

2. When Things Go South:
The Dark Side of Love

CONTENTS

Prologue

Three little girls were growing up in the world.

The first little girl became Miss American Sweetheart, a subservient Martha Stewart aficionado, overcompensating waifer-of-a-mind homemaker.

The second little girl, after a childhood of fighting to get to the top and breaking the rules in favor of her own, had a very different adulthood.

She is tough as steel filings, a take-no-shit bitch, uninhibited, unrestrained.

Like spit on a griddle, she's wild and real, ambitious and seductive – a go-getter who takes as many prisoners and lovers as she desires.

She walks tall, dreams big, and blows "buh-bye" kisses

with a wriggle of her hips as she exits the door, leaving the boys behind broken.

The third little girl was a combination of the other two. She grew up trying to decide who she wanted to be, what would push her to ride hard and stand tall, and what she could take make-it-or-break-it style from raw experience.

She combined the best of both worlds, and tempered every bit of devil inside with a little angel, enough so that it felt right.

That last little girl was me.

The Sun Rises East: Chasing Dawn with You

Drowning in the Shallows

I got good at going
To the shallow end of
Playing it safe in love,
Wondering all the while
When an ocean wave would
Make its way through
The body of water
And capsize me.

And still, I didn't want
A love that would wreck me.
I wanted loving hands and arms
To catch me instead.

The
Dance

Let yourself be pursued,

Let yourself be chased.

Once your desire has been filled,

Dance into the space.

Let yourself lean close,

And memorize his skin.

Peel off and glance back from the hall,

His eyes will tell what he let in.

— Did I leave an impact on you like you left on me?

The First Time

He said,

Nobody ever dances for me.

I thought,

No one ever dances <u>with</u> me like you.

Sangria
Shivers

Run your fingers up my hair,

Shivers down my spine.

Your words, your voice, even your stare

Taste like the

Sweetest wine.

more than
smoke &
mirrors

smiling, clasping for what it's worth,

every last bit watching it trickle down

pond-smooth like glass we're treading,

careful where we step apart –

aching fierce burning smoldering

up inside me hot chimney smoke –

too much to take, so just *take* me,

step up and bridge the gap –

everything you've been waiting for,

prove to me once and for all it's not

an illusion, can't won't go up in

smoke, flames, the we us together,

what's there will blow us apart to the

ends of the earth, start all over do it

again, just to have

your touch.

A Love Story
Better Than
the Movies

Is it always like this for you?
Because it's *never* like this for me.

– *feeling again*

Breathless

Wishes like ice,
Velvet slick to touch.
Running out of time,
Give a little nudge.

Water rivulets,
Beginning with a drop.
Waiting moment, infinite,
Breathless, my heart stops.

He Made
Time Stand
Still

Time she couldn't get back
If his heat didn't
Break through.

Can you trace shivers
Like mountains
Where she felt you on her skin?

Can you taste what it's like
To have left a mark
On another human's soul?

Dare
to
Dream

Run.

Run into my arms.

Run and make me whole.

I've waited for you ever since

My heart froze through with cold.

I know under the frost

There's still a girl who's lost

Her coursing veins and

Dare to dream

'Til she saw you and remembered it all.

only
you

inspiration soul-searing heat,

take me apart and put me back

together again with

skilled hands I'll blow hot and

you freeze me with ice cold shivers

'til I'm trembling, breathing in something

too beautiful for words, waiting, wanting

to scald you, tease you, tempt you into sin . . .

we're playing hide and seek and

it's one shadowy corner gone before I slip . . .

and stare deep into your eyes and

realize running from you isn't the same

as sinking deep into that hypnotic gaze

you give me 'til we touch palm to palm and

I gasp because overwhelmingly

it's YOU and only you.

Your Touch
Is Like . . .

Your touch is like

Poetry brushing

Fingertips

Tap tap

Across my Heart.

They Call You
My Achilles
Heel, But It
Doesn't Hurt
When
You Are
Here

They say you're my weakness.

You may just be my soft spot.

How could you know I was

Aching to rest?

It's like you were

Made for me.

hummingbird
wings &
butterfly
kisses

wide-eyed caught in the act of
looking up at you,
and it's never what you think.
the first glimpse,
and my ribs crack
under the strain –
heart beating,
hummingbird wings,
lifting me up for butterfly kisses,
here, there;
I can't get enough.
it soaks my skin in sunshine,
warm like your embrace,

as your arms encircle me,

and all I can call it is

home again

forever

with you.

Don't
Back
Down

The breeze blows in
And I don't back down.
I bare my face to the sun.
What used to scare me lies ahead,
I don't walk, I run.

I'm face to face with what I feared
And wanted all along.
Fluttering heart, dry mouth, knot in my throat,
I tell myself that I'm strong.

Enough to hold it together.
Enough to be self-contained.
I *shouldn't* fall too fast.
I should know better with age.

I could tell him how I feel.
I could let the light shine through.
I know I'm beautiful as I am –
So many feelings at starting anew.

What would it mean to let my heart in?
To be present and whole at last?
And stay with him in the moment.
Face my fears that it's moving too fast.

The breeze blows in and I don't back down.
I wait and stand my ground.
Looking for love and light in all the wrong places,
I finally feel found.

All I
Needed
To Know

Maybe I'm a girl
Who loved so much
And never wanted to let go.

That when I opened my hands
And breathed in love
I felt in my heart
All I needed to know.

The Kind of Magic Worth Waiting For

The magic with him is
Nothing like,
And far more than
Any poem.

There are butterflies, as well as
Desire and excitement.
And still, I find myself
Wanting to say
The magic lies with the magician . . .
But is that true?

Maybe he brings out the magic in me,
Like a musician drawing out music
From a violin or lyre.
Maybe the magic is between us
Like electricity,
Or the curve of a sway
When we dance
And my body follows
Like it's the only
Natural thing to do.

And maybe the magic is me,
When my smile, my words, my laugh
Tumble out and transfix
Those caught in my path.

That my heart, my vulnerability,
My playfulness, my depths
Can spill out and wash over
Someone like an experience,
A moment, a writing,
Or a mantra that
They were waiting for,

But didn't know the shape of yet.
Didn't know the taste of yet.

And maybe we'll get caught in
An infinity loop because
When I tasted you,
I knew I hadn't felt
Magic like that.
Magic worth waiting for.
Magic pouring out of me
In your presence,
And in the space between us,
Like a dare,
A voice saying,
There's more where that came from.

Is it any wonder then,
With the kind of magic act
I was exposed to when I was little,
That when I saw and felt
The real thing,
All these years later . . .

When you came to me
And stepped closer
'Til I couldn't tell where
The magic and you and I
Stopped or began,
It was all I could do
But to say,
"Yes" and
"I'm yours."

When Things Go South: The Dark Side of Love

Fifteen-Year-Old Heartbreak: Where It All Started

A glow, that glow, a wonderful glow,
It bathes me, caresses, with my heart it meshes
Into a tingle, that sigh, a shiver gone dry,
A trailing finger, a jump and a cry
Of shock and surprise, as you tantalize
And seduce young girls' minds
With those wicked blue eyes –

And that smile, it freezes,
My heart, oh my Jesus,
This sin we're caught in.
Innocence, incensed,
Burned away in the flames,
Is it really ordained?

That I'm falling, need saved,
Cresting a wave,

And that hold, warm deep,
One squeeze and I'd leap
For your every whim, your side games,
I was unbridled, then tamed.
And broken, a token, amusement and fun,
Finally armed with the truth, how from you did I run.

The promises broke,
But the lies never changed.
Every sigh that I gave,
Shove back into my cage.

Giving freely, heart flowing,
This heartbreak I'm towing.
Secrets I'm spilling,
The whisperers are milling,
Claiming my pain for their own eyes,
I'm trance-like, hypnotized,
Wondering where I've gone wrong,
Straining to hear song.

But instead bile's snatched forth,

"She's *different*, a whore!"
But only I know the truth,
I'm cold and aloof.
Trying hard to rise above the drama,
And all of it's from a
Boy who doesn't know what he wants.

Hungry
for
Love

Years ago, I said,

I am so hungry for love.
The kind that wrecks my world and
Makes everything I knew before
Pale in comparison.

In a way, you could say
I asked for it.

Rain is
Always
Welcome
in
Los Angeles

Rain is always welcome in Los Angeles.

I wish I was welcome, too.

Water flowing down your windshield,

My feelings are too much for you.

Too great for you to hold,

More than you deserve to have.

Brash, and maybe bold,

In the gazebo I hear the ringing of my laugh.

Too much in time,

Too much in time,

I've lost myself in you.

Idealized,
Idealized,
It's just this thing I do.

I can find Mr. Right,
In beauty anywhere.
But when I looked into your eyes,
I felt like Home had reappeared.

Too lost in time,
I'm lost in time,
The push and pull we danced.
Words don't align,
Words don't align,
I never hear why you can't.
I'm not enough,
I'm not enough,
Whispering for
Those in the back.
I need a sign,
I need a sign,
I can't source your presence
From this lack.

But just one night,

Just one night,

What I wouldn't give.

To dance and rise

And be alive,

You almost made me believe again.

Until She
is
Seen
Again

I couldn't wait

For you to remember

How you saw me at the start.

I remember the glint in your eyes,

Fervent fire in your lips,

And the chase,

Enough for us both.

I am statuesque in my stillness.

Desire fanned,

Curls falling like

Perfume in the air,

The vision you didn't even know that you missed.

Smoldering,

Enduring,

Holding heat in my embers.

Wanting, waiting,

Freezing,

Staying,

Until I am seen again.

Wanting More

I want to know what
It's like to touch myself and
Be left wanting more.

Black
Widow

Waiting on you
Is like
Holding my breath,
Watching flower petals unfurl,
Knowing that
The weight of my exhale
Could pin you
Like a spider's prey to her web.

These expectations in my chest
Are just a breeze and a buh-bye kiss,
From making me look like a fool
Who only spools out regret,
Waiting just to taste
What she couldn't get.

What black widows wouldn't give
To feel spring's victory.
The thawing of seeds remembered,
Outwaiting winter patiently.

She'd notice her thirst for something real,
Beyond her tangled net,
Of beautifully broken threads
Spelling out names she can't forget.

Veins laced with ready venom
To stop him in his tracks,
Can't do as much, the frost is back,
Defense is her last attack.

As she dangles mid-air,
Holding on to all that's left,
He comes from behind,
Finds heartstrings untied,
And devours her for himself.

He Put Me
Away for
Safe-Keeping
(So He Says)

Light dancing in your eyes,

Closed fist firefly,

Heat, damp, catch my breath,

Fog the glass, I trace your name,

Bubble in my throat, husky laugh.

Hands on your chest, desire fanned,

Sweet exhales, now light the match –

That you're holding, I'm aching,

Panted strains – not playing fair,

I'll meet you boldly, chin tilted, straight stare.

Hooded lashes, inky dreams, swirl the pot,

Fire spreading, legs coiled, my body held taut

In your hands, palms spread, I'm reaching for you,

The connection is dying, you whisper "Adieu,"

As you smile softly, put me on the shelf,

Where I can't have you, nor anyone else.

I Was
Made for
Impossible
Love

Make me do your bidding.
Take me for your own.
Rob me of my possessions.
My hands together sewn.

Waiting on your rhythm.
Throat and heart gone dry.
Wrists rub against the binding.
Rope biting as I try.

Hold this good girl hostage,
As you take your time.
Brown eyes sear me slowly,
Still can't read your mind.

Floating in the abyss,
'Til the end of time.
Anchored only by your kiss,
Unleash me with your sigh.

And at the end, it's what you say,
"I was made for impossible love."
Makes me turn my back on you,
Enough is enough.

Will
I
Ever
Know?

Part of me wants to ask – was it real?
Was it real for you?
Were you acting, feeling like you had
To please me or say
What I wanted to hear?

What happened after we left?
Did you come to your senses,
Find Jesus, and
Breathe better with me
Out of your system?
Did you forget how much
You claimed
I meant to you?

Did you move on,
Forgetting that I was
Still there?

Was it too good to be true,
For you, too?
Or was that just the alcohol speaking?

Poor communicator
Over technology that you are,
Would I finally get to hear why
If I saw you again?
Or would you hide
All the vulnerability
And parts of you
I tasted,

And bury them
For the right girl,
The right time,
When you felt better about yourself
And had that stability and identity
Men need to
Pursue and commit.

A belief that your career isn't ruined,

That you have that gift and

Potential I see in you,

That I wish you could feel, too . . .

A home, a path,

And some certainty

For yourself versus

The rug getting ripped out

From under your feet.

I want to protest.

I saw you knocked down and

I didn't run.

I saw you re-live a flashback

And I called your name,

Held and embraced you,

And let you feel my warmth

Until the past

Thawed out to

Safety, soft lips, and

Me believing you.

All I wanted in return was you,

Whatever you would

Freely give.

We danced by the beach, and
I was shyness,
Strappy heels, and
Wobbliness from
Drinks for courage.

And I was more.

I took chances,
Climbed atop you and
Drank from your lips like
It was the only sweetness
There was.

I laughed and played &
Felt you right there,
Giving back to me
Everything I gave
And more.

We swayed to salt and air,
And you held me,
Slowing me down.

You told me to
Just feel you,
And the music,
And just be here.
That just feeling was enough.
I did.

And I haven't been able to
Get the feeling of
You out from under
My skin
Ever since.

But at the end of the day,
My body is mine.
You had her for a night.
I have her for life.

In person you said again and again,
You are so beautiful . . .
You must know that,
Surely, right?
I laughed back and said,
Sometimes.

But I refuse to wait
For your gaze and words
To be what it takes
For me to remember
My worth.

Next time you say
You'll give me the world,
I'll tell you,
I already have my own.

I Can't Keep Promises After You've Left

Don't lose your sweetness,
he said.

But I can't taste it
On my tongue anymore
Since you left . . .

Seductress

I am soft rebellion,
Grace and grit,
Honeysuckle secrets flowing
through my veins,
Typewritten keys you have to
PRESS.

I am penetrating stares,
Soft curves you ache to follow
Like a siren's call.
Twisting, begging, trying to keep up,
Like if you ran faster
You wouldn't fall.

I blaze trails and frontiers,
Smoke plumes fanning from my chest.
Purple heather staining the sky,
Leaving pearls born from salt and tears,

You can *taste* in your mouth what's left.

Words you have to lean in close for.
Cursive shivers like whispers,
You're next.
You kiss me full well knowing
I'm a labyrinth with only one way out,
You're never getting me
Out of your head.

Ride
or
Die

Some people think of your 'ride-or-die'
As your person.
That someone who is willing to go
To Hell and back with you,
Loyal, ready, and at your side
As long as you are in it together.

I hear it, speak it, and taste in the words
A choice, a challenge.
Would you like to ride?
To go out of your comfort zone,
To feel the wind against your skin and
Live beyond what you thought was possible?
Or do you choose to close yourself off,
Stay small,

Stay in your lane . . .
Only to eventually wither and die?

What if you said yes?
But got off and realized
It was only a ride.

That you would claim that
Exhilaration and adventure
Like it was your truth,
A honeyed secret
More intimate than lover's breath,
That you held close to you and
Dipped into afterwards for sustenance,
Just a little bit at a time,
To make it last while
You 'got by' on ordinary.

Memories so vivid of
What it was like to be alive
Before you went back to
Just existing,
Before you realized your choice
Between the two

Was really more like
Stepping into a sequined dress
Dripping of desire,

And later, living in longing,
Remembering where there were
Imprints of sequins and hands
On your skin . . .
Versus living a lie
And never really knowing
What it was that
You were missing out on.

You can say yes again and again,
Trying to reclaim and trace your steps
To that moment you were asked,
Would you like to ride?

But amusement parks grow hollower by the day,
As your sensation-seeking nature
Experiences whiplash and overstimulation
Where delight originally lay.
You could spend the rest of your life
Holding onto a dream,

That you had no business wriggling into,
Forsaking reality's need

To show that you weren't in control,
And neither was he.
But if it was only just a ride,
When did it become the death of we?

If You Wanted Something Better

Go.

Go and walk the road.

Go feel the bare earth against your feet.

Go wade the river and let the water's current

Splash against your calves.

Go taste the sweetness of the berries

Hanging heavy on the tree.

Go to the forest and smell the expanse of

Clean, green dampness

And unspoken secrets.

Go and touch with tender fingers

The velvet petals,

Their curved stems,
And crisp leaves.

Just go already.

And I will, too.

Carbon
Copy
Love

I've lied about love,
Again and again,
Pretending this was it.

You pour ashes into
The setting of a
Diamond ring,
We all know
It's different.

Escaping
Your
Shadows

You struck a match
And lit aflame
Exactly what it was
I thought I wanted.

Until
Reality was snuffed,
And my dreams remained,
Flickering like shadows against the wall.
Mesmerizing those who still yearn to taste
Their own.

I could watch the dance for hours,
The way the light teases and entrances
Darkness

Beyond a curved ever-changing shimmer of a line.
"I want you. Now, I don't."

I can't even see the
Rise and fall of the sun,
Can't feel the warmth of hands extended,

Asking softly
To pierce through the shame with light
And get that girl out alive.

Begging, a reminder now,
To say yes and live once more.
Can I keep it?
I want to know.
Yes, I can keep my heart,
And its propensity for wanting what it can't have
Until it heals
The light and shadows
Within.

The candlelight flickers as I pour out
Soft black clouds of steam and
Rainbow-kissed oil drops
Down the drain.

They weren't fit for consumption, but
Who really knows when
I'm swilling down drink,
Haunted by that
Smoky deliciousness you brought,

Forgetting you pair best with
Empty promises that
Couldn't sate the hunger of a
Girl starved for the other half
And range of human experience.

She deserves it all.
She can find it all.
But this means dropping deadweight,
And letting go of trying to fix those
Who can't love themselves whole either.
Who try and shape and mold women
Into their 'missing piece,'
But do not do the work
To become that for themselves.

If there's anything I know, it's this:
I can't compete with an image, memory, or shadow

Of the woman you think I should be.

But I can create my own dance of light and dark,

And even if you're left behind,

It won't matter because I'm free.

If I
Can't
Let You
Go Now

Falling into darkness,
Reaching for the walls,
Clutching at the passing air,
The urge to end it calls.

As my spirit fights,
Intent on holding tight,
I grip it harder
Knowing that
This can't be my life.

Moments flash before me,
Culmination of it all.
Ragged breaths, adrenaline

Held in, too tight, too long.

Rushing wind,
Ears closing in,
I know it as I fall.
If I can't let you go now,
I'm never moving on.

Choices
(It's On
the Menu)

Everyone wants to feel something.

We all get a choice in how we find that feeling.

I Can't Quit When You're On My Lips

Why does a bad habit like you

Have to taste so good?

Frozen in Foreplay: He Made Time Stand Still (Part 2)

Tick.

She holds her breath.

Tick.

His fingers climb.

Tick.

She's frozen to the spot.

Tock.

He tells her,

You're mine.

Tick.

He's so unhurried.

Tock.

He likes to take his time.

Tick.

Beneath his hands, she's thrashing.

Tock.

Beneath his smile, he's lying.

Unmoored, she wakes up,

And her limbs become hers.

What a dream, *he's a dream*,

But inside she's torn.

Time.

Give me time.

Give me time and I'm yours.

Hear my sigh,

Feel my hips,

Take your time and explore.

Frozen still,

Like before,

Rooted there,

To the spot.
Was it everything you wanted?
Did you want
What you got?

Give me time,
He whispers.
You had your time,
Now it's winter.

Frozen in time, she waits.
Trembling in cold, she endures.
If it was a dream, it wasn't real,
If it wasn't real, he wasn't hers.

Time she couldn't get back,
Until his heat broke through.
Desire pools slow and heavy,
Breath held for answers like clues.

Can you trace shivers like mountains
Where she felt you on her skin?
Can you taste what it's like
To have left a mark
On another human's soul?

Can you finish what you started,
Make her come alive again?
Or will you bury all the parts you let her see,
'Til the right time, the right girl?

Do you always feint with fire?
Are you scared of getting burned?

He replied,
My touch would burn you up,
Make you combust,
When will you ever learn?

Tossing her head
And licking her lips, she said,
I think I'm finally heated through,
I'm <u>ready</u> for my turn.

The Sun Sets West: He Left Glass Shards Behind

Betrayed
by
Sheer
Belief

I wished deeply

With all that I had left in me

For love that would never come.

For You

I wept for you.
I wrote for you.
I binged for you.
I wished for you.

And still I slept alone.

I caged ragged sighs for you.
I tried on for size the truth
That you were really gone.

I walked in a fog of numb.
Watched as my life came undone,
Straining for the words of our song.

I sat silently on the shelf,
A forgotten doll left to console herself,
All I had was holding on.

Porcelain cracks ran rampant through my veins,
Couldn't put myself back together again,
I was broken beyond repair.

Jaw clenched, holding in tears unshed,
Living life hollowed out from what you did,
I drowned in my own despair.

I set fire to burn down all that I loved,
Flames licking the words, "She was never enough"
To keep you after all that I did.

Charred remnants of moments that carried me through,
Living off memories, heart fluttering,
Like when I was with you,
But ashes are all I have left.

I dreamed of you,
I keened for you,
Held onto us,
I screamed for you,

But you wouldn't grab my hand.

I prayed for you,

I waited for you –

Cut myself down to be

The girl slated for you

. . . But that might mean you were never really my man.

Running
From
What
You
Can

Every problem you have is one that could be solved . . .

But since you can't run away from those,

You'll run away from the one that you can:

Me.

My
Only
Witness

At some point, he won't take up
So much space in my head,
So much claim to my heart,
So much ink from my pen.

Each word betraying trembles
From a girl who held her own,
But fell deeper
Than she ever planned.

Splayed against
Cream white pages
As her only witness.

Broken
Promises

Promise me the world,
And all that you can't give.
In the end I'm strong enough
To love you just for trying.

Glass Shards

Them: *How did you get that scar?*
Me: *Let me tell you all about it . . .*

I smile from behind a glass wall.
What can't be touched
Will not be broken,
Contrary to what you thought.

I cannot feel the cracks
From outside
Etched in your shaking hand
And lukewarm attempts at rejection
(ending *this*).

I am encased in steel, breathing fog onto glass,
And writing my own ending,
Finding the words in my voice that
You didn't have the courage to say.

My heart can't swell beyond the confines
Of a manufacturer's warranty past its
Expiration date for caring,
But it does its best.

Too late, but in time, it reminds me that I am
Protected from risks like men
Who leave glass shards behind.

But going against my last words –
I am a prize, and you no longer
Get to have access to me –
In the form of walking back to you,
Cuts me in places I didn't even know could bleed.

I would bleed for love.
I would bleed for tasting your truth.
I would bleed for:
*stolen moments
*honeyed kisses
*the moon as our guide,

But I will not bleed for you.

It All
Sounds
Like
a Lie

He left so my life could come together
And something better could fall into place.

Will I
Feel
the
Same?

Will I feel the same
When I see your face again
After all these years?

I Once
Fell in Love
with Weather
Like This

I once fell in love with weather like this.

Felt my trembling inside against the fullness of your lips.

You say you'd throw it all away, if only for my kiss.

Looking at the city lights, I see the sky from the abyss.

I see the stars framing us against the backdrop of night.

Gripping your jacket with my hands,

Holding on with all my might.

I'll never let you go, and I'll always be your light.

But my darkness always wins, you say,

It won't go down without a fight.

I took a chance long ago in weather like this.

Trading in my good sense for fall air so brisk,

That each breath reminded me –
This is what it's like to be alive.
You saw and had to have the
Girl with stars dancing in her eyes.

We lived a lifetime of love in the hours of a dream.
Where I was too much and not enough,
And your demons roamed free.
We had it all in our hands, but nothing comes for free.
I lost myself in you, and you couldn't
Find in the mirror
The man you used to be.

Desert beauty tainted black,
Tarnishing the memories of we.
Trying to trace amongst the ashes
What was left of all our dreams.

I'm on all fours in the soot,
Was this how you wanted me?
Trying to put back the glass
You broke in order to *show me* how to be.

I held onto the man I loved
Who couldn't find his inner light.

He claims he lost me to betrayal,
Though I never left his sight.
I whisper to him softly that it will be all right.
Even when his head is turned,
I stay through the end of night.

I breathe in, and breathe out,
And I make a little wish.
I run my hands through his hair,
Stroking back the silky wisps.
In his arms, I'm with the stars,
But when it's dark, he's holding me
By my wrists.

I pray that when I next call it love
That it doesn't ever feel like this.

I used to think that I had found
My forever in weather like this.
Until after the storms all I had to show were
Bruises laced with his kiss.
I said I'd never let go, and I'd always be his.
But when I see the stars tonight,
I know that I deserve to live.

Filling
the
Void

All this time spent on
Filling the emptiness of you
That I can't even be present
With myself anymore.

Depression

I am a robot with no feelings.
I can't remember what it is to have feelings.
I am stiff and surprised by wet eyes.
What is there to cry over?
Lancing through my cheeks, my jaw
Pulls my mouth down slack.
I am the Lion, Tinman, and Scarecrow all in one –
Except I am the body without a voice,
The therapist with a mechanical heart,
And the poet with a dull brain of cotton.

My stomach is round. I used to care,
But these are trivial matters.
I am not looking anymore, and neither should they.
I drag my feet forward . . . backwards . . . it is all the same.
There is no compass.
The Earth is round, as well.

I end up where I started and cannot see what is before me.
The horizon flatlines, like my heartbeat and pulse,
With that break in landscape, in reality,
Cutting me off from the rest of the world.

I hear laughing, but I can't tell if
What's being said is funny or not.
I remember the vibrating hum, the bubbling tinkle, and
Rich timbre of my own laughter in my throat.
It is so far back down now, leagues below,
Leaving behind red gutted lines of
Dehydration and aching sadness that
I try to coat with forced swallows
To smooth when I speak.

I am often tired. I fly high at work,
A kite soaring to inspire and lift up others,
My turquoise ribbons beating in the breeze,
Touching the sky.

I am in it so deeply, the method actor of Oz,
But the wind is knocked out of me as I walk out the door,
And I feel relief, slipping off my gingham dress at home,
Tucking it tenderly into the drawer until

The MGM fantasy of tomorrow begins.

And I could tell myself again and again in a hollow tone,
There's no place like home,
until I'm there without purpose, back to what
should have been my refuge,
before I realize the tornado is not something
that touched down –
It is something I carry inside me that
unleashes at the familiar.

It is every bad dream I can't wake up from,
Every separation from my loved ones
Whom I thought I lost,
And the dropping of my heart at having come this far,
And believing as truth what the man behind the curtain
Says I am, and all that I am not and can never be.

It is the recognition that I can't have back
That magical feeling and love from having helped others,
Making connections so beautiful with people
On their healing journeys and
Finding inside
What they thought

They lacked all along.

At the end of the day, the feeling disappears.
I lose that hope that I held for and with them.
Clicking my heels together,
Saying like a prayer,
There's no place like home . . .
But it hasn't felt like home since he left.
I can't bear the present, so I try and go back to that time.
But clicking my heels, imagining his face,
Doesn't undo or erase the mundane.

Maybe it was enough to have lived it – to have dreamt it.
Maybe I lived another life in that fevered dream,
And that's all I can ask for.
Maybe the vivid colors and richness of Oz are
My only saving grace,
My way to imbue hope
Into a world of gray and
Tornado black.
Maybe it is up to me
To breathe color into the reality
I woke up to and
Am left with now.

I'm
Not
Ready
Yet

I'm Not Ready Yet:

How to protect yourself from

Ever having tried.

Kelebek
(*Butterfly*):
To Have and
To Hold
What Was

It is hard to be loved when your sadness
Piles down on you like the sand
From a smashed hourglass,
Spilling over all the dreams and desires
You built up overlooking the tide,
And burying the girl you used to be.

Your face is covered and if you open
Your mouth to scream,
All you will taste is glass,
Breaking down into granules.
Because time heals all wounds,
But only if you keep your mouth shut

To keep the avalanche from caving in.

You can't see or feel
The sun's rays kissing your freckles,
Burnishing your hair with a soft glow.
You haven't had that since the last time
He traced your skin and left tingles on your arm,
As your lips sought out sustenance
To make it through the goodbye.

You replayed the tenderness of
Those final moments,
Treasuring them with a sweetness like
They were a butterfly cradled within your
Hands aboard the flight home.

You made it home, but the butterfly
Was left behind,
Dying behind oval airplane windows,
Promising the beauty of a life together below.
And the butterfly, holding onto that vision,
Breathing in that manufactured air until
There was not enough fantasy
Left to subsist on

Until the plane landed.

You got off not where you thought you would,
But became an island beholden to an era
That not even the locals could make sense of.
While they live their lives and bustle
Back and forth between
The sacred and the mundane,
You stay beneath it all, and carry the
Weight of remembering, for you, and all of
The others who have had their wings clipped.

Loving him gave you wings, and once
Upon a time, all your work had given you
The strength to move them.

But losing him shut down the world
You had begun to believe in,
That you swore would never be built
Around a single person.

And as you lay still, feeling the ocean's
Sway beating on even after death,
You question whether the weight pressing
In on you is sand,

Or a protective cocoon you built
To keep others from seeing your pain.

You have tasted the depths of
Your own abandonment,
And left yourself surrounded
By a wall of numb.

You wait. Time will tell.

A butterfly is stronger than a castle of
Sand that washes away at high tide.

Trapped inside her own prison,
Her thrashing and
Wings beating will be for naught.
She will feel forgotten.

But reborn from pain, healed through the
Safety of her own making,
She can fly out
The window of that castle
Before her life is taken.

She can let the sunshine

Illuminate the wisdom of
The writings on her wings,
All the images in her mind's eye that
She couldn't find the words for.

And she will sing her story high above
In the sky as she makes
Her way home, and
Back to who she knew she was
Before when she felt free.

She Had It All

She had it all
can no longer be
the battle cry I bellow
In protest of living in this world.

Waking
From a
Nightmare

The real nightmare
Is waking up
And not being able to
Turn to the
Person you love.

Cast Iron Heart

If my heart was cast iron,
After I cast you away,
But found a way to hold on,
You'd be beholden to me and stay.

I've had a stake in our love affair,
But it wasn't fair of you to leave.
I can't believe what you have done,
What you haven't is let me grieve.

Grief gave me strength, but at a cost,
Accosting me through the night.
Clad in the nightie that moonlight seeped in,
I remember the girl you liked.

The girl you strummed guitar to,
And sang clear through the chord,
Cleared out the doubt in my chest
That this was going to hurt.

The way the laughter rumbled in my throat,
Rich and throaty up all the way,
Makes up for all the moments passed,
Time passed since you went away.

You went where you thought you belonged,
Where I longed to be by your side.
Yet you saw ahead where I could not,
You felt called to let our love die.

Back and forth calling me names,
A more callous state
Than you'd ever been in my arms.
Armed with vitriol and hate,
Cultivated for months,
I took it as penance for lies I'd led on.

I couldn't take it back at the beginning.
Nor before we were committed.
Not even when the room was spinning,
Or you yelled that this was ending.

It didn't matter that I was afraid,
Or that I'd been faithful to the promise of you.
Because you couldn't get over from the start
What I did before I was ready to choose.

You couldn't expel from your heart
The tornado of imagined men of, 'Who's who?'
You compared them all in your mind,
I wanted to save us without losing you.

The man that I loved went down with a fight
Against his darkest self.
I carried the darkness to breathe light back in,
But couldn't get out myself.

Away from the shame and out of the guilt
That I held onto to be close to him.
Closing in on myself, and what was there left,
But a girl quivering on the shelf.

And they ask me what happened,
To that girl standing powerfully,
That brought the boy in with dazzled eyes,
A cast iron memory.

The Greatest
Mistake
of All

My greatest mistake?
Believing that I didn't have
Anything to say.

Seeing Beneath the Magician's Cape with The Eyes of a Child

Saying that I am a survivor

Is as foreign to me

As speaking about

A time or two I went to the circus,

And declaring to girls mauled by beasts elsewhere,

"Yes, I was there. I was in the audience.

I agreed to come onto the stage, each time I was asked."

But the magic lies with the magician,

And the Keeper of circus animals caged.

And it is hard to say you take much

Home from the circus

But a memory or two.

But my life changed? My world rocked?

That came from the time my mother told me
That I didn't need any more food,
That I had had enough already.

That came from the boy I loved from
Halfway across the world telling me
He no longer wanted to be with me,
And stars dancing across my eyes,
My tears blurring their outline and
The shimmer making them dance faster,
Before they finally combusted,
Leaving my world pitch black.

My life felt rocked when I circled from
The mirror, to the scale, to the kitchen
For food to stave off the onslaught of
Fear and being out of control,
Until I lolled in a food coma,
Staring up at the ceiling,
Thinking about what I had done.

They tell me that those things are connected,
And a part of me says yes, we are and everything

Is all connected, except for the fact that *that*
Is a blip on the map, and can something that small
Have led to all that?

I try to make sense of the abstract word 'trauma,' and
The horror and helplessness often tied to it
Ringing hollow to my own truth and experience.
I grasp on to the bits I can make sense of,
Like having my personal and physical
Integrity of self violated,
Which makes sense,
Because I found it difficult to reconcile
As a teenager how I had made it to third base
And knew how to give head
Before I had ever kissed a boy.

And while it never crossed my mind
Except for testing the boundaries of friendship
While dutifully recounting with
Girl Scout fingers in the air
My secret,
The last league signifying that this was a *true* friendship,
I have rarely walked out of a training on
Childhood sexual abuse

Without having had my eyes grow wide
To keep the tears from
Springing forth and outing me
Amongst my peers.

Is it worse because it happened in my bed?
While my parents were gone and I was being baby-sat?
Is it worse because I laugh at my silver lining punchline of
The story, and some audiences give me unwavering
Angry stares of disbelief?
Is it worse that I can't remember more than two times,
And maybe that means I blocked out more,
Or is that better,
Because that's all there was,
And I didn't feel forced
And that explains why I feel golden and well-adjusted
Compared to the others?

Is it worse because when I confronted the
Person who did this,
I was met with confusion and calm,
The other voice clear and genuine that
This never happened,
Unless it involved us taking an innocent bath together

Or something of the sort?

Is it worse because despite my family culture of
Open communication and
Family dinners,
Always being there for each other, and
Seeing my parents' loving faces at sporting events . . .

We never talked about it when I was growing up.
And the only reason I knew that *they* knew
Until I was 12 and
Brought it up by my own volition
Being that, at age 6,
I told my friend, who told her mom,
Who I *heard* tell my parents,
With my cries in fear that I would
Be in trouble drowning out
The words of my friend's mother
As she said
What I couldn't to them.

I am perfectly happy and content to say that
It wasn't my fault, and
I don't blame my six-year-old self

For wanting to go along and please her baby-sitter,
Because others speaking well of and
Acknowledging her
Made her heart swell up
And feel whole.

I do have a part of me that wants to say,
So what?
I am more preoccupied with the
Sense of emptiness
I carry in the present –
Scratch that, that keeps me from
Fully being in and enjoying the present,
And that I get stuck on
'Surface-level topics' like *my body* because
I want the world to see me like I once saw myself.

I want to find ways to express and create and
Consecrate my purpose with a higher power, and
Live fully as I was meant to . . .
But that shatters when I look in the mirror or
Put on clothes and see and feel my weight adding
Rolls and smudges to the self-portrait of
Someone whose soul has

A radiance and inner flame unmatched.

Each time I get caught up in
Sensations and waves
Rocked forth by food,
I feel myself tamping down and
Almost snuffing out the flame
That burns bright and
Reminds me daily of
Who I really am.

I hear you telling me that love has to
Start with myself.
Not by setting up hoops to jump through,
Not by a diet of self-hate and denigration,
But by living in and occupying that space of
Acceptance as if I am already there.

But I can't dance freely as I do in my dreams,
Baring my soul and my curves
Like a feast for the world.
I can't walk the Southside streets
With my head held high,
Hips swaying back and forth,

Catching your eye,
Because I get a blank stare back,
And it's been a while
Since I felt my
Pulse course as I drink in
Your gaze with my smile.

Since I had that power and influence
That I always tie to thinness,
That lifts me light and free
As I pull them closer into me.

But maybe it's all connected.
This performing and pleasing has
Left me affected,
And empty, afloat,
Alone on the boat

In a sea of self-doubt,
Trying to cast out
The girl who wants too much,
But is never enough.

I weep for her struggles.
I hold her pain.

I swallow her sorrow
Again and again.

And she needs to know that I trust her now,
That I know she knows best.
We can't worry about the others,
Lay their expectations to rest.

And I feel her in me,
The little girl calling my name,
Seeking out pleasure and truth,
Who dreams of fame.

And past aside, I nurture her so fully,
She won't know what hit her,
The strength of my love unsullied.

And if I have her on my side,
I have wisdom and grace
And forgiveness unrivaled –
That sees beneath the magician's cape
With the eyes of a child.

And I won't let food or choked words
Tear me apart and

Turn on myself.
My body, heart and mind are one,
I take care of what's left.

Placing
Her
Bets

And after so long
It was herself that she should
have placed her bets on.

Salt
Trails

I can't waste any more tears

On a future that

Will never happen with you.

The Body
I'm Living In
Isn't
Mine

The body I'm living in isn't mine.
I wasn't robbed, held at
Gunpoint in a deserted alley.
I wasn't threatened.

I let go of non-essentials,
Taking only my heart and mind
To the battle frontlines.

I couldn't see, anything but
What was right in front of me.
I ate to survive, and to feel
Some semblance of control.
I only had my own arms

To hold and to soothe me.
Instead of turning to myself,
I ate to quiet, to numb,
And let the warm rays of
Temporary peace and contentment
Run over me as
Full and steamy as
An ever-running shower.

I didn't know, or didn't want
To see what was behind
The fog of the mirror.
What I had become.

I touch my body with damp hands,
Sliding down pockets and
Mounds of flesh
That conquered all the lovely lines
And valleys of my figure.
Flesh rolling over itself, streaked with
Bruise-like stretch marks that
Worked overtime
To accommodate
The vastness of my pain.

I tell myself stories, and look
Away from the ravages of my
Former beauty to understand what is left,
How I lost
Who I thought I was.

I hold in my palms
Quicksand slipping
Through my fingers,
The things I couldn't grasp.
Love, the love of my life.
My body, my beauty, my smile,
Adorning me like a scepter crafted
For the reigning queen.
Hope, assuredness, of my place
And future . . .

Slipping faster than my fingers can close.
Loss.
I ball my hand into a fist to
Make it stop.
I squeeze air and hold hard,
Like I can save it for my aching
Throat and lungs.

There is nothing like what I
Had before, as I unfurl
Tear-streaked knuckles and
Grubby fingers open.

I held on too hard, too late,
Living in the past,
Dying in the present.

I breathe.
I see me in the mirror.
My eyes well with salt and tears.
I know who I was,
And see the resemblance.
But it is so much,
Too much,
Maybe more than I can bear.

This heavy body,
Weighty flesh,
And trembling lip,
Trying so hard to stay strong
Without bending or bowing
Under the weight of

All her shame.

I step away and rinse my hands,
Tuck my hair behind
My ears and pause to
Touch my throat.

'Loving him gave her wings,
and all her work had
given her the strength
to move them.'

That girl he loved, that she loved,
Is still there. I am her.

Massaging lotion to her fingertips,
Unfurrowing her brow and
Picturing the heavy heart
Beating, even still,
She promises:

I will love you.
I will find you.
And find a way
For you to come back

And co-exist in
This space with
Pain and me.
There is enough room
For us all.

We have tasted
The sweet,
Choked on the bitter . . .
But stayed hungry for
Passion, and open
to adventure.
It is time to try
And love again.

What
Is
Yet
To
Come

She held in her hands

The most beautiful sunset

That lit the night aflame

With what was yet to come.

Healing Where There Was Hurt:

Finding My North Star Home

All
I
Have
Left

All I ever wanted
Was to let out the
Breath I held inside
Thinking,

I am all that I have left.

I didn't know yet
This mantra
Would be my
Source of strength.

My
Saving
Grace

My head said,

I'm tired of transmuting pain to purpose.

My heart said,

This hurt is too great to bear.

My hands said,

We can't stop now,

And kept writing until

From the pages,

A landing nest appeared.

Finally, I could

Lay myself out and

Have softness meet

My jagged edges,

Like the salty ocean spray
And holy steadfast waves
That heal even as they hurt.

The Birth
of a
Heroine

I used to cry in the car when my face was too dry,

Like cracks of imperfection marring

The mirage that I was getting by.

My dad didn't understand that my face was so tight,

I needed moisturizer to breathe.

Reminding me that I'm soft skin

And filling up the well that wants to please.

I want you to want me,

Vanity was once a gleaming sword.

That I unsheathed and backed away from

Into the makings of my own world.

Where all I am and all my worth

Is what you think of me.

I will play the part to my own death,

Distracting them so as not to leave.

I am flesh, I am heart,
I am brains and bravery.
And now, I am fat,
Starring in a tragedy.
Where I give up, but not my act,
You must see more than what I've lost.
For what I've gained is how to numb –
Welcome to my crash course.

I want you to see me love,
How the light frames me when I smile.
Where I steel my resolve, and
Go forth the extra mile,
In my journey as a heart warrior,
Helping others rewrite how they see themselves.
As my pen stays stuck, I'm out of ink,
I've nothing left for myself.

But if you can carry hope for me,
I'll tell you in my spoken word.
The story of a girl who lost herself,
But held onto her sword.

She uses it not to fight,
She played that game for far too long.
She traces a circle in the dirt,
And lilts a haunting song.

Of joy, of trembling fear,
Of shame and desire alight.
Free from self-degradation,
All she wants back is her life.

Something molten, something real,
Something created just for her.
Something strong and forged with steel,
Healing her wholly where it hurts.

A locket over her heart, holding
The pieces she thought she'd lost.
And the ink she had run out of,
Waiting to write her life's work.
The locket opens, like her to the world,
Sharing her authentic self.
Not what she thought they wanted of her,
But more than she thought was left.

Her voice began as soft and small,
Whispering through the mountains
Like the wind;
She sings the joy of her own truth,
No holding back or feeling forsaken.

She left her mark on the world
In a circle traced in earth.
And at the center of it all,
We witness a heroine's birth.

The Medicine

Don't get bitter.
Just get better.

Remembering Your Worth

You are a woman of value.
If he makes you forget that –
Forget about him.

And if you can't do that yet,
Breathe into that space
In your chest
To make room for
The part of you
That remembers
Who you are.

She is Me,
I am Her

It happened to me today.
Reading and re-living
The last love story I ever knew,
I felt all the feelings –
the adoration, humor, teasing, & intimacy.

I looked through photos of me
Going out on the town,
Standing on tiptoes to kiss him on
The cheek like he was mine,
Laughing with my head tossed back,
Linking arms with friends,
Reflecting back a girl who had
Full roses for cheeks and white teeth,
Like she was sparkling from within.

When I looked up, I felt different.
I remembered who I am.

I am the girl who is filled with joy.
Who takes risks and is
Open to the terrain of the unknown.
I saw the pictures, and smiled knowingly,
Thinking, *She's cute.*
But she's. Still. Me.

That girl is there beneath some pounds.
The weight does not have the
Power or strength to
Quell her spirit.
She is enchanting.

The boy I loved may
Have brought her out,
But I am more delighted and centered
On making her acquaintance,
As much as I enjoy the witty banter
And written form of their (then)
Budding love story.

I can appreciate all the things
That led to her falling for him –
His heart, his mind,
His kindness & quick wit . . .
Even his sadness, and
Especially his vulnerability.

But, too, I am transfixed
By the woman made more beautiful,
Unencumbered and free,
Through the
Power of his attention.

I remember her.
I remember being in her body,
Residing within that space,
Experiencing the magnitude of
Her ability to captivate.
Her relishing of being deeply seen,
And her blossoming from
Having been witnessed.

She is a goddess,
A wholly raw and feeling human being,

A child's innocence,
The warrior's shield,
And the lick of flames of fire
Restoring hearts and hearths.
She is a menace to reckon
And a sight to behold.

She is me. I am her.

I am the whisper of wisdom
Soothing and grounding
The wielding of her
Mighty sword.

I am the mother,
The parent,
Lovingly tucking her
Curls behind her ears,
Fresh-faced and ready
To change the world
Through the power of
Owning,
Being,
Exactly who she is.

She grew into her own,
Blooming from the love,
Encouragement,
And greatly destined dreamer ideals
Of a boy who loved her –

But the tendrils of ivy
Breathing green magic,
Like the wisps of curls in her hair,
Were meant for more than ivory towers,
And beyond castle turrets
Standing guard and gatekeeper
To the princess-pipeline dream
Of being rescued by a prince.

She is the forest,
Sighing softly
And enduring beyond
The hum of the city.

She is the mossy green carpet expanse
That lines promises unspoken,
Where the wild things dance.

She is the place you go and reveal

Your deepest secrets to in the mountains,
With the reverberations of echoes beyond,
Speaking the truth of your heart,
What you yearned to say all along.

She is me. I am her.
The world is her oyster.
Possibilities, her earth.

The Beat
of My
Heart

They ask me,
Why do you dance like that
When there is no music?

I tell them,
It's okay –
I carry the beat
Inside me
Wherever I go.

Garage
Sale
Goodbyes

Is it really goodbye
When you leave behind
All the layers of you
No longer needed for protection?

Everything thrown down in disarray
From thick-plated suits of armor
To barely-there brittle sheddings like snakeskin,
Containing a kaleidoscope of feelings
Under the microscope
That is also on the floor of things left behind for *more*.

Pieces that served their purpose,
That I have tried on
And worn through seasons,

My second skin,
Only to be shimmied out of
And dropped like a silk robe
Unveiling a woman
No longer afraid of herself.

I am bare
Of all my excuses, defenses, reasons why –
I can't, I shouldn't, this won't work out,
And my favorite –
I don't deserve this,
My unsung truth of time.

Traded for footsteps forward
On a path that I can
Only see through feeling.
My body, my heart, my throat,
Urging me onwards
To the *more*
I always said I had to be good for.

Crooning like a lullaby,
Yes.
Yes.

Yes.
I get to keep me, with all of my
Wisdom, heart,
And strength of mind.

Yes.
I didn't need to be perfect,
Only willing to let myself
Be seen whole.

Yes.
I have been waiting for this.

Yes.
I'm finally free enough
To let in the *more*
I held off for so long.

All it took was saying *YES*
And betting that
I am enough
Exactly as I am.

Wanderlust

She had wanderlust so full
It overflowed
Like fresh rainwater after the storm.
Her heart smoothed over with mud,
Patching all the cracks
To hide where it was torn.

Looking
in the
Past

Looking in the past

Doesn't let me see

The fierce and graceful woman

I was always meant to be.

On Love

Loving someone and being loved is like a blueprint, map, and memory of who I am at my best. Giving and receiving love has been my greatest compass, richest experiences, and best lessons of all time. All these years later and I am still fiercely exploring and learning to stay open, live in grace, and remember the ability I have to deeply love. You helped me realize that what I thought was my greatest curse is actually my greatest gift.

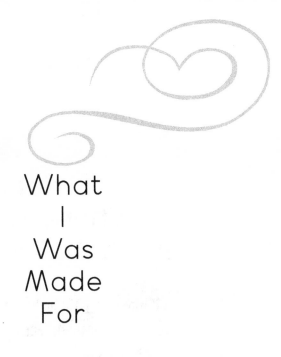

What
I
Was
Made
For

I was made to move mountains.

I was made to love.

I was made to impart and

Be the change

I wish to see in the world.

I'm Not
Where You
Left Me

I'd like to say I'll be here waiting,

But in all truth,

I don't want to tell a lie.

Here, home, now, before, etc.

As reference points are

All arbitrary,

But we use and rely on them

Just the same.

All I know is that I will be

Stretching, striving,

And fighting

For the glory of

My own love,

And seeking that

Inner peace.

On Knowing
That I
Deserve
To Be
Powerfully
Loved

Being powerfully loved . . .
Means not having someone negotiate down
The amount of time you spend together.

Being powerfully loved . . .
Means being admired, respected, held,
And unafraid of others
Seeing and knowing this.

Being powerfully loved . . .
Demands recognizing and acting
From a place of

Being worthy as you are,
And not some conditional bar
To be met first.

Being powerfully loved . . .
Means not having to apologize
For speaking your truth.

Being powerfully loved . . .
Is the balm for your soul
That helps you rise up and
Keep going until
You believe in
Yourself again.

Being powerfully loved . . .
Is transformative,
And has the power
To leave you irrevocably
And forever changed.

Being powerfully loved . . .
Means you wholly matter,
In spite of,
Or maybe even because of

Your shadows, flaws,
And wounds.

Being powerfully loved . . .
Should imprint and stay with you
As a reminder that
You deserve to be treated
Like the goddess you are.

Being powerfully loved . . .
Is a gift, a legacy, and an unfolding
To a lifetime where you
Get to make the choice
Of falling in love
With yourself again,
Each day anew,
Because you knew others loved you before
Like it was the
Only choice there was.

Breathe
in Beauty

Breathe in beauty,

Cast out the doubt.

Breathe in beauty,

Then let it out.

Breathe in beauty,

Cascading strength.

Breathe in beauty,

Your light's aflame.

She Can Fly

I can't give up on me,

Just because he did.

I need to love me,

Even if he won't.

Because he let me go,

I can now soar.

I'm untethered, untangled,

As free as a bird.

On Sisterhood

I am so full,
Replete with love,
Sisterhood stretching
Me wide open,
Touching my lips, tasting
What I'm like when I'm
Glowing, wide-eyed,
Heart spilling over
With belly laughs,
Shimmied hips,
Fire and soul.

Veins flowing, alive,
Refusing to bend or fold
For disappointments
That might have
Tried to break me before.

This is what it's like
To be sated again.

Embracing

Waking up
And embracing what is
Loves and nourishes me
More deeply
Than trying to hold onto
What was
Ever did.

Glass
Bottle

If I could bottle this feeling,

For all the hungry girls out there,

And my younger self,

Still nibbling on breadcrumbs,

All of us insisting that we really *are*

Quite full,

I'd let them each catch

A drop on their tongue,

To taste again magic,

And remember that it's real.

To remind them, and us, and me

To not settle for anything less than

Safety and butterflies

Mixed together.

Getting to breathe into our pores
That warmth and nurturance
Of being enough,
And having another delight in that.

Where we once tried to
Cover up our scars and
Stuff our stories,
Having someone touch and
Trace the outline
Of what made us who we are.
Earnest, soft, and persistent,

To taste, hear, and feel
Who we became.

That we could arrive imperfectly, and
Captivate,
Magnetize,
And draw in
Someone else's depth and yearning
Simply by standing
Knee-deep in our own.

Salt water tasting like tears,

Like a new day,
Like I could get sun-drenched
And taste the richness at high tide,
Uniting with a kiss in the sea –

No, this tastes like *victory*,
And hope and wildflowers
That can't be stomped out.

Water waves carrying
Our love, resilience, and
Bravery for burning brighter,
Fragrant like a field
Ablaze in fall colors that
Dance like fire.
Held, pressed, and
Leaving something
Of substance behind.

Loving stained fingers
Like an artist
Dipping into her palette,
Making something out of nothing,
To a tincture and a balm.

Bottled up, sealed glass,
Ready to nourish,
Able to outlast,

'Til it reaches women and girls waiting
To know they are enough
Exactly as they are
Right now.

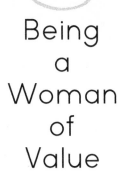

Being
a
Woman
of
Value

Being a woman of value

Stakes me like roots

To the ground,

Wreathing me over

Through and through

To my fingertips that graze the stars,

Filling all the spaces in between.

There is no room left for self-doubt.

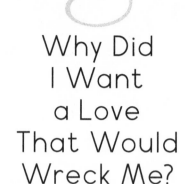

Why Did I Want a Love That Would Wreck Me?

Why did I want a love that would wreck me?
Why can't I have a safe harbor?
Why can't I have loving hands
That hold me when I'm fragile,
And a love that breathes
Through and with me
Until the storm passes?

Why can't I have a love
Where we laugh and dance
And crackle
Beneath a sea of stars,
And instead of getting

Burned by the heat,
I'm warmed inside out,
My heart beating a
Happy rhythm,
Saying yes to this
Forever?

– *Asking for what I really want*

The
Promise

Fear of abandonment?
Whatever it means to you,
Don't ever abandon yourself.

Don't
Give
Up
on
Love

Let the dream change, but
Don't give up on the dream.

Like a potter at the wheel
Letting the clay change shape,
Too, let your fingers run
Messy and juicy
As grapes on the vine.
Squeeze out what you
Always wanted,
And delight in the taste.

Humming softly,

Getting lost in the flow,
Let loving fingers hold
What is yours,
What is meant for you,
Believing with sweetness
It will always find you.

Thrash and pulse and see
What fate puts before you –
When you pour passion
And sweat into what matters.
When you dare and
Call it art.

Trace the fault line
With your big toe,
Riding the uneven edges where
Inspiration and destiny meet.
Catch your breath at
The gap in the middle,
Where there is nothing
To hold you
Except for chance singing,
Keep going

Until you make it to
The other side.

Don't ask where or what
Or how or why NOW
This very moment,
You deserve the thrill of
Something real beyond
Your wildest dreams.

In a world teeming with
Possibilities,
There may be other,
Important questions to ask.

Namely, what's stopping you
From saying yes
To this moment,

And who died
When that old dream
Gave its last sigh
And told you
That you couldn't have
What you really wanted?

Lump in your throat,
Lump of clay in your hands,
Creation of something out of nothing
Like the pen that you grab –
Say yes to getting onto the ride
Without knowing the end.

Throw caution to the wind
Like a fist full of dirt to the sky.
Let the pebbles make their mark
Around you
In the outline of a crown.
Let your wildness rejoice
And climb over
And through you
Like vines on the ground.

Let the dream change, but
Don't give up on the dream.

Ode to My Untamed Heart

And haven't you heard by now?

I'm a lioness,

Not a lamb.

Little Girls and Dreams Never Die

I've never forgotten the way my heart opened to you.
My edges bending like a willow in the wind,
Soft and caught in the gust of you.
Ready to follow you to the edge of the Earth,
And back again, because
A circle never ends.

Seeing you always brought up that tingle in my throat –
Breath held, holding back possibilities
Like butterflies and scattered seeds
Just waiting to touch down
'Til I'm home in your arms.

I couldn't ever get rid of your strumming of guitar,
Singing sweet melodies, counting stars.

I climbed into your lap, and you held me there.
Like I weightless, and yours,
Undone by your stare.

I landed in a nest of almost more than I could bear,
The sweetest love,
What I feared.
Saying yes to getting hurt,
Losing myself.
I wanted you badly,
And still I was scared.

You were everything to me:
My future, my lover, my adventure partner;
my dreamer, my cheerleader, my man.
We'd travel the world and create a life together,
But the ink on that dream dried up as it ran.

What do you know of the seasons?
What do you know of the tides?
What do you know of the beach you showed me,
Where you said you'd someday propose to your wife?

I knew it wouldn't be me.
I knew I couldn't hold you.

I eviscerated my self-worth
If it meant buying time
'Til we were through.

I'm sorry that I lied.
I'm sorry you were hurt.
I'm sorry about your pride,
As you drank in my past
With a sordid thirst.

I'm sorry I held you captive.
You couldn't escape the pain.
I loved you with all my heart,
But you held up a mirror to my shame.

I want to hold that scared boy
So desperate for love,
He'd burn down the world with
His very last match
If it meant he was enough.

That impressionable young boy,
Abandoned at boarding school –
Even when he begged,
His parents wouldn't stay.

Who learned his mind was a refuge,
A weapon forged in the fire,
To protect when he felt afraid.

Touching palm to palm
Is my little girl,
Hungry for love,
Wanting to be seen by the world.

No one had seen her before,
Quite like him.
Touching, tracing
Down his palm's heart line,
And he, leaving forever ripples
Where his fingers skimmed.

Touching only through the heat of their fingers,
Tip to tip.
They were changed.
Tip to tip,
And she couldn't go back.
In the briefest touch, she saw it all,
A dream she didn't think she could have.

So much intimacy,
Touching only tip to tip.
Less than a year of her life,
Fueling what she wouldn't give,
To have him back again,
Loving him wholly where it hurt.
Healing her own wounds,
And remembering her worth.

Into me you see.
I thought I needed you.
I never saw me again
With quite the same view.

I don't believe in your vitriol.
I won't hold your hate.
Cutting me down like shredded
Ribbon of something you loved,
In a language I barely speak.

I loved that sweet little boy
With his shy smile and curls askew,
But the kind of healing love he needs
Can't come from me, only you.

And my little girl
Singing her heart out
to a sky full of stars,
Lit up with wishes,
Fevered dreams,
Tracing constellations
From her scars.

It's time to let go of the dream she held close
Of running into you.
The key to her heart,
Unlatching a chest to
The future she thought she knew.

One city and two worlds,
Reunited at last.
Moving towards adventure,
She'd still be chasing at best.

Far apart and then near . . .
Losing you would be worth it
If you finally appeared.
Losing me
could have been worth it,

If you wiped away the tears.

I have so much life still
To unlock and to live,
It's a shock I still carry
Any dreams of you left.

But little girls and dreams
May never die,
They change and they transform
From a lover's sigh,
To holding her own
Bated breath,
Stoking the fire, awakening
A blaze from what's left.

From longing to hope
To cherishing now,
She kept on moving, even when
She didn't know how.

But little girls and dreams
May never die,
They change and they transform,
From You and I
To Me.

Signed,

The Woman Who Won't Give Up

On Loving Me Free

If I Can
Make It Here,
I Can Make It
Anywhere

Hope blossoms from once-scorched earth.

She's finally found her way.

Epilogue

When she got her first journal, her first diary,
she marveled at the space she had. All hers.

Just for me.

Larger than the size of her hand, hard plastic pink
with a bit of sheen to it, and spiral-bound,

Like it could hold something of substance.

Cotton candy with magenta-outlined shadows on the
cover, and some tracing of a black unicorn.

It felt like her.

Innocence on the outside, like a sweet dog you could
pat on the head before passing on by.

But inside the cover, splayed out on those pages,
were her innermost thoughts.

Musings, a gently budding 'til-the-vase-tips-over kind of
rebellion, a little fire, and deep –

Like a well that stretches until it meets the water's edge –
Kind of longing to be noticed.

Everything she could see, that she knew and saw and
took in but didn't say was right there.

If they only knew, they wouldn't pass on by.

They wouldn't be able to help but stay.

She asked herself . . .

What do you want to write about?

She dreamed and wondered and thought.

About love, redemption, second chances,
and rising from the ashes.

About a star of a woman who refuses to let go of her
sense of wonder and stares out boldly at the world.

About capturing that moment in which she fans out her
fingers and with practiced ease, watches the ashes fall . . .

Knowing that she has room to finally have it all.

Acknowledgements

THANK YOU SO MUCH to any and all those who have supported my growth as a writer, a therapist, and a human being. Particularly to anyone reading this book – I am thankful and owe so much to you – the readers, the writers, the dreamers, the fighters, and to those who took chances like it was the only choice there was. I am forever inspired by you.

Thank you to some of my very best friends spanning California, Pennsylvania, and Kentucky – Mallory, Meghan, Alyssa, Janel, and Kathleen – you mean the world to me, and I am so grateful for us to get to witness and love each other into these next chapters.

To my Louisville Loves – Kayla, Laura, Christie, Leah, and Gabby – I love and appreciate you, your patience, your inspiring journeys, your drive and commitment to your dreams, and for your unconditional love.

So much gratitude to my mentors who have supported me on my writing journey - Cheryl Ades, Carol Lozier, and Dr. Patricia Jabbeh Wesley.

I'd like to express my deepest thanks to Zoe Bird for her support and guidance in the editing of the initial drafts of my manuscript. I am grateful for her loving feedback, clarity, and wisdom that helped this book come into being.

Thank you to the University of Louisville Kent School and Couple's and Family Therapy Program that helped to shape so much of who I am. I am so lucky to have made incredible connections with my cohort, mentors, colleagues, professors, supervisors, and co-workers who came through and after this chapter in my life.

Special thanks to my post-graduate licensure supervision group with Dr. DeMarquis Clarke, particularly Michaela and Gina, for helping to love me, challenge me, and help me grow.

Thank you to my University of Michigan Sex Therapy and Sex Education Cohort, for all of your support, love, humor, and wisdom. Thank you for inspiring me and showing what can happen when we give ourselves & others permission to explore our deepest desires and aspects of who we are. "Talking about sex will change the world."

Healing has meant allowing pain and trauma to move through me, and to reclaim the body space that is mine.

Thank you to my Body Kindness and Plus Size Women's Empowerment Group in Louisville and to the Yinz Bopo Group in Pittsburgh for helping to promote unconditional love at whatever shape and size my body is – that I am deserving and whole as I am.

I am so appreciative of the friendship, fierceness, laughter, and *carpe diem* way these groups have helped me and so many others to live life freely and on our terms in a plus-sized body. As a sisterhood, we support each other, take chances, have adventures, and create a safe and loving space to show up as we are – all whilst combatting fat phobia, body shaming, and internalized beauty standards.

Thank you to my volleyball and dance communities, particularly my tango family, that have helped me to fall in love with what my body can do, express, and create as I gave myself permission to be embodied and do what I love again.

To the men whom I loved, whom I lost, and who taught me so much – thank you.

To Shahram – Thank you for helping me to believe in love again. I experienced love within my family; I believed in love with and for my friends; but I didn't know if I was capable of falling in love again. You are someone who challenges me, makes me laugh, inspires me, dazzles me, and makes me feel safe and cherished.

Giving and receiving love with you has been life-giving, and means more then you could know. You helped re-awaken the part of me with a wild & untamed heart, and me being brave enough to follow wherever she takes me. If I had my way, I would say yes to forever with you. *Atashe delam*, I am so grateful that I followed my heart so that it led me to you.

To my family – the McEachrons, Utechs, and Thweatts – I am who I am because of you. Thank you for loving me, supporting my dreams, encouraging me, and for creating a family culture and legacy of laughter and love together.

Thank you to my brother, Mike, for his help in creating a website that allows me to connect with others through my writing.

To my parents – Mom and Dad – you have been there for me through everything. I love you so incredibly much, and am grateful for your support, and in awe of how you each lead through example in the ways you unconditionally love and show up for each other and me.

I am also infinitely grateful to have been connected and to have gotten to work with Christine Horner, The Book Cover Whisperer, for all of her help in the creation of my book cover and the interior design. Thank you for bringing 'my baby' to life with gorgeous imagery, and for all your love and time.

Special thanks as well to Anelise Patton of Withering Muse for hand-crafting the map that weaves together all the chapters, leading to the treasured prize of *The Place That Keeps Love Alive*.

Coralie Shawn McEachron

CORALIE IS A WRITER AND POET whose day job includes helping people to find healing where there was hurt before, in their relationships with themselves and others. She is a Licensed Marriage and Family Therapist and Certified Sex Therapist, as well as speaker and presenter.

In her free time, she loves to dance tango, belly dance, and hip-hop; play volleyball; read; play with her puppies; and spend time with loved ones and family. She resides in Louisville, Kentucky, and has lived all across the country, including Columbus, OH; Los Angeles, CA; Houston, TX; and Pittsburgh, PA.

Her favorite place in the world is Istanbul, Turkey, and she has studied Turkish, Spanish, and now Persian language. Though she has professional qualifications and loves her work as a 'heart warrior,' writing poetry is a form of self-care that allows her to connect with others on the same level, as someone navigating the human condition. Her work is dedicated to finding strength through vulnerability; freedom through surrender; grace in our mistakes; and healing through pain transformed to purpose.

Credits

Rain is Always Welcome in Los Angeles
This poem was written as part of a contest on Instagram, using the final line of Yesika Salgado's poem "Metro" from her latest poetry collection, *Hermosa*, as a ghost line. I have a connection with having grown up in Los Angeles and loving someone from there, as well, which tied in with the inspiration for this poem.

Will I Ever Know?
This poem includes a a variation of a quote by Monique Duvall, that I would like to give attribution to as the paraphrased version of her quote appears at the end of my poem. Duvall's original quote is as follows:

> "He offered her the world,
> She said she had her own."

Ride or Die
This poem is inspired by and in part response to the Bill Hicks' sketch, "It's Just a Ride." So much profound wisdom is found in this piece of work.

Kelebek (Butterfly): To Have and To Hold What Was
The Body I'm Living In Isn't Mine
From the book, *Matched*, I want to give credit to Ally Condie for her beautiful line that appears in its original form or a variation thereof in both the above poems:

> "Loving him gave me wings and all my work has given me the strength to move them (p. 60, *Matched*)."

What I Was Made For
This directly includes at the end of the poem a quote often attributed to Mahatma Gandhi: "Be the change you wish to see in the world."

It should be noted that some sources state that he did not actually say this, but that rather, it is paraphrased from his original quote:

"We but mirror the world. All the tendencies present in the outer world are to be found in the world of our body. If we could change ourselves, the tendencies in the world would also change. As a man changes his own nature, so does the attitude of the world change towards him. This is the divine mystery supreme. A wonderful thing it is and the source of our happiness. We need not wait to see what others do."

– Mahatma Gandhi

Don't Give Up on Love

This poem was influenced by Langston Hughes' poem, *Harlem*, particularly with the rich imagery used to explore what happens to a dream deferred. There are also elements in this poem that draw inspiration from one of my favorite poems, *The Invitation*, by Oriah Mountain Dreamer.